Ek Aonkar

A leader will Rise
A leader is needed
That leader is you!

H.S. Puri
7/18/21

H. S. Puri, PhD

Second enlarged revised edition

Children's book

The book is a part of *Selfless Seva* (community service) by the author and not for any monetary gain. There is no copyright for it but acknowledgement will be appreciated.

PREFACE

During the British rule in India, *Om* was translated as *Brahman*, which in Indian mythology is the creator of the world and hence is somewhat like the Christian God. The earlier translators of Sikh scripts into English equated *Aonkar* with *Om* and hence *Brahman* (God). In *Gurbani*, the creator has been described as *ekam* which stands for *Ek Aonkar* - unique, without duality, and a formless entity. *Par Brahman* (Akal Purakh, beyond creation) is also considered *Ek Aonkar*. Some scholars think *Ek Aonkar* to be just a logo - a sign for one God.

With these developments, the common translation of *Ek Aonkar* became "One God" or "God is one", which is popular even now. When investigated in detail, some intellectuals gave the views that it is an auspicious mysterious word, beyond the comprehension of a common person. It defies all meanings and explanations and it should be taken as such.

In this book for children, the background of *Ek Aonkar* is given in simple English based on facts and not from hearsay. In the case of *Gurbani*, instead of word to word translation, transliteration of the verses has been given to convey the real meaning to young readers. Wherever possible, non-English terms are given in **bold** or *italic* letters to differentiate them from the English. These terms have been described in simple English so that the children understand what they are reading. As Guru Nanak Dev Ji said, "*Gaviya sunniya mann rakhiyo bhav*": Sing, listen and understand the meanings.

H. S. Puri, PhD

Table of Contents

Introduction

੧ੴ ਸਤਿਗੁਰ ਪ੍ਰਸਾਦਿ
Ek Aonkar Satguru Prasad *(838 - 18)*

- **Ek Aonkar** represents One unique, universal Creator. One absolute reality. A gift by the Eternal Guru.
- **Sat** conveys the meaning that in the beginning there was the mere state of **Sat** (truth), which was beyond time, immutable and without the second.
- **Guru** here is a giver of wisdom. It is a combination of **Gu + Ru. Gu** means darkness and **Ru** means light: "One who brings from darkness to light (knowledge)". There is no one greater than Guru. It is He who grants us divine knowledge.
- **Prasad** is generosity and bestowing of boon by Guru as a gracious gift (**Ek Aonkar** is a gift of **Satguru**). Now it is a religious offering in the form of a sweet preparation (**Karah Prasad**).

ਏਕਮ ਏਕੰਕਾਰੁ ਨਿਰਾਲਾ
Ekam Ekankar Nirala *(838 - 19)*
The One universal Creator is Unique.

ਅਮਰੁ ਅਜੋਨੀ ਜਾਤਿ ਨ ਜਾਲਾ
Amar Ajonee Jaat Na Jaala *(838 - 19)*
He is immortal, without birth or death.

ਅਗਮ ਅਗੋਚਰੁ ਰੂਪੁ ਨ ਰੇਖਿਆ
Agam Agochar Roop Na Rakhiya *(838 - 19)*
He is Formless, invisible, and is without shape or figure.

ਖੋਜਤ ਖੋਜਤ ਘਟਿ ਘਟਿ ਦੇਖਿਆ
Khojat Khojat Ghat Ghat Dekhiya *(838 - 19)*
I googled Him everywhere.

Chapter 1
Beej (Seed) Mantra

Sri Guru Granth Sahib Ji means:
- **Sri** - glorification.
- **Guru** - giver of wisdom.
- **Granth** - a religious book.
- **Sahib** or **Sahib Ji** (Master) - a word of respect for the superiors.

Sri Guru Granth Sahib Ji starts with **Ek Onkar** or **Ek Aonkar**. It is a **Beej Mantra**. **Beej** means seed and **Mantra (Man+tra)** is an instrument to positively transform thoughts in the mind. It keeps the name of the Almighty in our mind. It is a word for concentration during recitation of a sacred utterance with spiritual powers.

Beej Mantra is said to be the starting point for divine knowledge, as given below:

ਬੀਜ ਮੰਤੁ ਸਰਬ ਕੋ ਗਿਆਨੁ

Beej Mantra Sarab Ko Gyaan *(274 - 16)*

Beej Mantra provides knowledge to all.

In **Beej Mantra, Aonkar** is a seed force that evolves as one of the sources of knowledge of the universe. It is a core **Mantra** with great spiritual power. Some people call **Aonkar** as **Ongkar (Ong+kar),** which is a **Sanskrit** word that means great. It has also been described as the "truth of the creator's creation", who is beyond birth and death. Both these terms also mean subtle divine wisdom or infinite energy.

(In the Western world now, ONG is an abbreviation of "on God" which means "I swear to God").

Normally the **Beej Mantra** stands for a single word. But in **Aonkar, Aon** and **Akar** combine together to form one sound so it can be considered a **Beej Mantra**. Regular chanting of **Ek** and **Beej Mantra (Aonkar)** combine together to form **Ek Aonkar**. This enhances spiritual power by decreasing confrontation and worries. It is also called **Beej Akshar** (seed word) - a letter for **Param Atma** (Supreme Soul). The meaning is subtle and mystical.

Beej Mantra leads to **Mool** (root) **Mantra**. It is just like the next stage of seed which when sprouts develops a root and gives rise to the whole plant.

ਅਉਖਧ ਮੰਤ੍ਰ ਮੂਲ ਮਨ ਏਕੈ ਮਨਿ ਬਿਸ੍ਵਾਸ ਪ੍ਰਭ ਧਾਰਿਆ
Aukhad Mantra Mool Mann Ekae Mann Biswaas Prabh Dhaariya (675)
Mool Mantra is the only one medication that enables the faith in Prabh (Supreme Being, Master) in our mind.

ਮੂਲ ਮੰਤ੍ਰ ਹਰਿ ਨਾਮੁ ਰਸਾਇਣੁ ਕਹੁ ਨਾਨਕ ਪੂਰਾ ਪਾਇਆ
Mool Mantra Har Naam Rasayana Kaho Nanak Pura Paya (1040)
Guru Nanak concludes that Mool Mantra is a tonic (rejuvenator) for union of the self with the Divine Name of the Creator.

Chapter 2
Sri Guru Granth Sahib Ji

The commencement of recitation of **Sri Guru Granth Sahib Ji** starts with **Ek Aonkar**. Here **Ek Aonkar** is used as **Mangala** or **Manglacharan** meaning auspicious, which was very popular during the time of compilation of **Guru Granth Sahib** in medieval India. It was a special practice that promoted the accomplishment of planned work. It was an invocatory formula, a symbol for welfare and happiness, and considered a blessing from the Almighty. Common people used it as a greeting in any writing material, particularly on the top of a letter or a religious tract or before writing the first alphabet on the first day of schooling. Its representation now is the first word **Orha** in the alphabet of Punjabi script for **Ek Aonkar.** The old **Gurmukhi** did not start with **Orha**.

In our homes for our regular recitation, we have a small book, which has some selected verses written by our Gurus. When a book of **Gurbani** is small, it is called **Gutka** or **Pothi.**

Gutka Sahib Ji

The most common **Gutka** is **Nitnem** which means daily routine. It starts with **Japji Sahib** (Punjabi: ਜਪੁਜੀ ਸਾਹਿਬ) and is a devotional recitation for individual wisdom. **Japji Sahib** was written by Guru Nanak Dev Ji in simple Punjabi and it comes in the beginning of **Sri Guru Granth Sahib Ji. Jap** is the recitation of verses again and again. **Japji Sahib** enlightens us that there is only one **Kartar** (Creator), and He is a reality. He is called by many other names in the verses of our Gurus. No specific name can be given to the creator as He is above all. He is indescribable (viz, can not be described or discussed). He is **Anant** (timeless).

In **Nitnem, Japji Sahib** is followed by **Jaap Sahib** (Punjabi: ਜਾਪ ਸਾਹਿਬ). It shows the virtue of **Waheguru,** which means, "*Hail the great Guru, wonderful sovereign*". **Jaap Sahib** was authored by Guru Gobind Singh Ji and **Dasam Granth** starts with it. **Jaap** means to utter with complete devotion.

The other type of popular **Gutka** is **Sukhmani Sahib** (Punjabi: ਸੁਖਮਨੀ ਸਾਹਿਬ) which means "*Prayer of Peace*".

ਸੁਖਮਨੀ ਸੁਖ ਅੰਮ੍ਰਿਤ ਪ੍ਰਭ ਨਾਮ
Sukhmani Sukh Amrit Prabh Naam (262 - 13)
Sukhmani is a way to immortalize the name of *Prabh* (Supreme being).

Amrit is **A+mrit,** meaning the one that defies death.
Naam is a divine name, the word of divine knowledge and wisdom. The bliss of the great mind.

Sukhmani Sahib deals with topics such as **Simran** (recitation that leads to merging with the Almighty) and **Naam Japna** (meditation). Meditation of **Naam** is also taken for the greatness of Gurus and **Sadh Sangat** (holy congregation), true devotion and doing good deeds.

In **Guru Granth Sahib,** we commonly come across **Ek Aonkar Satguru Prasad**. Here **Satguru** (self realization) is a physical form of creator. **Sat** is **atma** (truth and self). Truth emanates from reality. It is what is real and what exists. According to Guru Nanak Dev Ji, **Satguru** is truth itself and is not a physical entity. He is the one who liberates us from worldly sufferings by His blessings (**Prasad**), because He (Guru) has liberated Himself from these.

Chapter 3
Childhood of Guru Nanak Dev Ji

The word **Nanak** earlier meant celebrity. **Dev** means divine, and **Ji** is used at the end of the name for distinguished persons, so Guru Nanak Dev Ji means "Divine celebrity".

As a child, Guru Nanak Dev was very inquisitive. At the age of seven, a teacher started teaching Him 35 alphabets of an old type of **Gurmukhi** (a common language at that time) in the usual way. But Guru Nanak Dev Ji linked each word of it with spirituality as given in **Raag Asa Mahala** 1, **Patti Likhi**. Later on he was taught by a teacher of **Sanskrit** called **Pandha** (short form of **Pandit**) and a teacher of Persian language called **Maulvi**. They considered Guruji as a common student. They could not detect in Him the wisdom, the spirituality, the deep philosophical thoughts and lack of interest in materialistic things.

Pandit (**Hindu** priest)

Moulvi (**Muslim** religious man)

Guruji's father was managing a big agricultural estate, so he had to deal extensively with the labour, farm products and the money matters. He wanted his son to be an efficient manager in dealing with these trades and also an expert in book keeping by learning accounting and business.

But the Guru had much higher ambitions. He had a philosophical aptitude. He observed that doer is unknown but there is action. He was particularly interested in knowing about that Creator and the other secrets of nature. To find out the answer for these, he even meditated in a river nearby for a couple of days but he could not get a satisfactory answer. He was looking for some learned persons who could understand what He wanted and quench His thirst for knowledge. In His hometown, the religious persons who were supposed to be enlightened had limited knowledge, which could not satisfy Guruji.

Chapter 4
Journeys of Guru Nanak Dev Ji

When disappointed at the state of affairs existing in His home, Guru Nanak Dev Ji decided to move out of His hometown and travel to other places in search of knowledge. He wanted to meet the learned, knowledgeable people who may have the right answers to His queries.

He got a very good companion Bhai Mardana, who lived nearby to His house. Bhai Mardana was a simple, innocent man but he was very good at playing **Rabab** (a music playing instrument like a violin). Bhai Mardana accompanied Guruji at all the places and remained with him till his last moments.

Rabab

During His several visits to many parts of India and abroad, Guruji discussed about the mystery of Creator and Creation with various learned men, scholars, sages of all the sects and high priests of both the **Hindu** and **Muslim** religions.

At the time of Guru Nanak Dev Ji, and at some places even now, people were not aware of the true nature of the Almighty who is an ultimate reality which is something that is superior and final. This fundamental power is all reality. The ignorant people were misled by the so-called religious men everywhere. Every preacher had his own concept of whom to worship and in what way, for a happy, healthy life, for mental peace, prosperity, salvation and forgiveness of sins.

Pandits had their scriptures in ancient Indian language **Sanskrit** while **Maulvi** had their religious book **Quran Sharif** in Arabic language which came from Arab. The majority of the population could not understand the scriptures of either of these. All these religious men were far away from reality and did not know themselves the mystery of nature. They would explain various natural phenomena on the basis of mythology or by some cock and bull story. There was a reign of darkness, ignorance and intellectual bankruptcy everywhere.

The common masses were moving from pillars to post for the right directions for peace of mind and calmness. But they were faced with charlatans of religions everywhere, who cheated them by faking astronomical calculations and providing them with talismans etc.

Guruji not only gave His sermons in the language of the people but also warned them about those religious people who glorified themselves by various rituals and visits to religious places on pilgrimage. They made their physical rituals a very holy affair but mentally they were totally unholy.

ਨਾਵਣ ਚਲੇ ਤੀਰਥੀ ਮਨਿ ਖੋਟੈ ਤਨਿ ਚੋਰ
Navan Chale Tirthi Mann Khote Tun Chor (789 - 9)
Going for pilgrimage with an evil mind and bad intent

ਬਾਹਰਿ ਧੋਤੀ ਤੂਮੜੀ ਅੰਦਰਿ ਵਿਸੁ ਨਿਕੋਰ
Bahar Dhoti Tumari Andar Vis Nikore (789 - 10)
From outside like washed gourd but from inside full of poison

Some of these religious men worshipped deities carved from various metals, stones, wood or other living and non-living things. A poet once said that there were so many gods and goddesses that there was no place to stand on the earth. As per ancient Indian scriptures, their number is 33 crore (330 million).

ਕੋਟਿ ਤੇਤੀਸਾ ਖੋਜਹਿ ੩ ਕੳ ਗੁਰ ਮਿਲਿ ਹਿਰਦੈ ਗਾਵਣਿਆ

Kot Tayteesaa Khojeh Taa Kao Gur Mil Hirdai Gaavaniaa *(130-13)*
**If you are looking for 33 crore gods and goddesses,
find them in your heart with the help from the Guru.**

If a devotee wanted to recite the name of the Almighty for peace of mind, the religious preacher would say, "*One should go to a solitary, isolated, peaceful place like the jungle to be near to the Creator*". The other would recommend going to a pilgrimage "*Have a dip in some river particularly Ganga*". Some conveyed the idea that worship of a particular tree, monument or graves of old sages is the best place for this.

Lady worshipping **Shiv Ling** made of stone.

Guru Nanak Dev Ji discarded all these notions and the other **karm kands** (physical activities for worshipping without using any knowledge) and laid stress on understanding and reciting the only One unique entity **Ek Aonkar** at any place at any time. He advised ignorant people why to go to jungles and far off places for peace of mind and to look for the Creator which gave us life. He is always with you *all the time*. You can remember that Almighty *at any place*.

ਕਾਹੇ ਰੇ ਬਨ ਖੋਜਨ ਜਾਈ

Kahe Re Ban Khojan Jayee (684 - 14)

Why do you go to the forest in search of Him?

ਸਰਬ ਨਿਵਾਸੀ ਸਦਾ ਅਲੇਪਾ ਤੋਹੀ ਸੰਗਿ ਸਮਾਈ

Sarab Niwasi Sada Alepa Tohi Sang Samai (684 - 14)

He is present everywhere and is always with you as your companion.

Chapter 5
Writing of Patti (Wooden Board)

Patti Likhi is the first sermon of Guru Nanak Dev Ji during his admission to the school. He mentioned to His teacher that the One who has created all the existence is the sole Lord of all. Success is only achieved by those who stay focused and are clear about their objective. Learn to stay on track for the purpose of life. Understand the world where you live.

Later Guru Nanak Dev Ji wrote all these teachings on **Patti** (wooden board) as during those times, the writing papers were not available everywhere. Before writing, **Patti** was glazed with a fine layer of clay paste made by mixing clay with water and then dried. For writing, hard reeds of grass were used as a pen. The reed was cut on one end in the shape of a cone.. With this pen, writing was done with a black ink (called India ink now). This ink was prepared by mixing a very fine powder of a wood charcoal with the gums of a tree and water.

Sometimes the papery bark of a tree called **Bhojpatra**, growing in the high Himalayas, was used as paper. This bark is thin light brown in colour and is curly so it was stretched before writing. For very auspicious scripts, a solution of saffron in water was used as ink for writing on it.

Picture of wooden boards

Original **Patti** of Guru Nanak Dev Ji.

Gurdwara *Patti Likhi* Sahib near Nankana Sahib,
where Guru Nanak Dev Ji received early education.

A picture of the present day **Patti.**

Patti and pen

Chapter 6
Multiple Ways of Writing Gurmukhi

Earlier **Gurmukhi** was written in multiple ways as depicted in the pictures below.

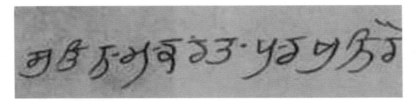

Mool Mantar in the handwriting of Guru Har Gobind Ji
in a *pothi* kept at the Amritsar Museum.
Note that A (ਾ *maatra* in **Gurmukhi**) is represented by a dot.

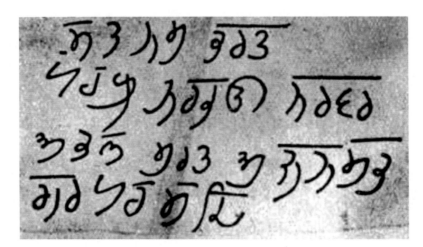

Mool Mantar written by Guru Har Rai Ji (without *maatra*, no vowels).

The original **Ek Aonkar** written by Guru Nanak Dev Ji could not be obtained but we have on record **Ek Aonkar** written by other Gurus.

Ek Aonkar in the handwriting of Guru Arjun Dev Ji.

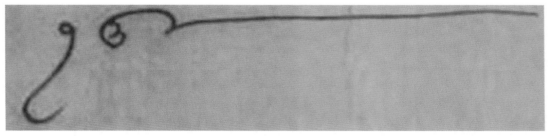

Ek Aonkar in the handwriting of Guru Har Gobind Ji in a **Pothi** (notebook) kept at the Amritsar Museum.

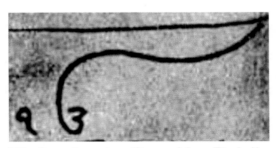

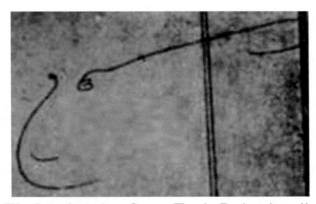

Ek Aonkar by Guru Har Rai Ji.　　**Ek Aonkar** by Guru Tegh Bahadur Ji.

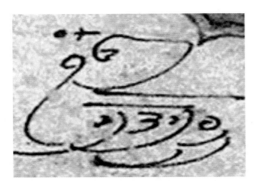

Ek Aonkar in the handwriting of Guru Gobind Singh Ji.

Handwritten Ek Aonkar in 1915.

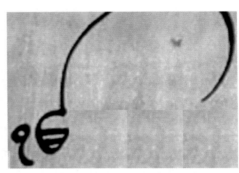

Opening page of **Guru Granth Sahib** in 1934.

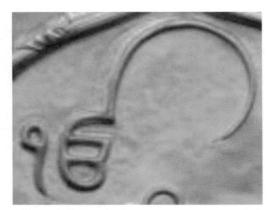

Ek Aonkar at the **Darshani Deori** (main entrance) leading to the pathway to the Golden Temple.

Japji Sahib in old **Gurmukhi**.
In this writing all the words were joined by a single line.

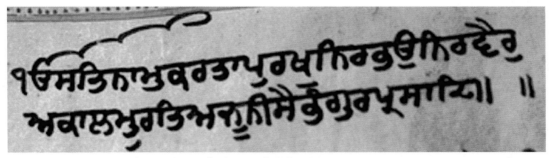

An early way of writing **Gurmukhi** where a sentence was written
without gaps between the words.

Many other persons as per their own imaginations have also designed **Ek Aonkar** in their own ways.

Ek Aonkar from an old book showing **Akalpurukh** in the numerical One. In **Orah** starting from the top are **Vishnu**, **Brahma** and **Shiva**.

Various forms of **Ek Aonkar.**

Variant logs of **Ek Aonkar.**

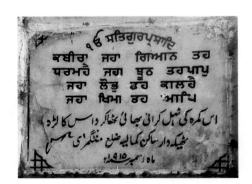

Ek Aonkar on a marble slab engraved in 1910.

Chapter 7
Explanation of Ek Aonkar

What we call **Ek Aonkar** today is a mysterious word and we do not know its exact meaning and pronunciation, as it has been available to us only in written form since olden times. The detailed description of **Ek Aonkar** is only available in the writings of Bhai Gurdas Ji.

Bhai Gurdas Ji was a Sikh scholar very close to the Fifth Guru, Guru Arjun Dev Ji, the compiler of Granth Sahib. Regarding **Ek Aonkar,** he mentioned that it was created by itself. This is unique, immortal, unborn, without cast and family. According to him, Guru Nanak Dev Ji came to the conclusion that it is unique without a second. Five Gurus one after the other composed thousands of hymns in praise of it. It is the figure of **Satgur Purakh** (One who knows the unseen lord). **Ek Aonkar** is the Lord of the entire creation, who existed before the creation and who alone will survive the creation till the end.

Bhai Gurdas Ji explained **Ek Aonkar:**
- *Akaunkar avar nahin dooja Nanak ek samai*: Guru Nanak came to the conclusion that *Ek Aonkar* is unique, without a second.
- *Oankar adi, kathni anat*: *Ek Aonkar* has been there since a very ancient time and there are numerous explanations of it.
- *Onkar utpati kiya din sabh raati*: *Ek Aonkar* gave rise to day and night.

Bhai Gurdas Ji has given numerous spellings of **Ek Aonkar** in **Gurmukhi** at different places in his work. For example, *Ekam Ekankar, Aakamkar, Eckankar, Akankar, Eckankar, Onkar, Oankar, Akaunkar, Ekamkar*, etc. His conclusion was:
- In the beginning, it was formless (viz, only a sound with no written representation).
- Later, it got the figure of **Eckankar.**

- Bhai Gurdas further said that it came into being in its complete form by adding one to **Aonkar** (union of **ekam** with the figure **Oorah**).

Even during and after the time of Bhai Gurdas Ji, **Ek Aonkar** has been written and spoken in various ways. In **Guru Granth Sahib Ji**, at some places, it is written as **Eckankar**. A sect of Sikh priests called **Sant Samaj** use **Ackankar** for **Ek Omkar** or **Ek Onkar**. Its short form as **Ekamkar** is also common amongst Sikhs.

Guru Gobind Singh Ji gave the following views about **Ek Aonkar**:

ਪ੍ਰਥਮੇ ਓਅੰਕਾਰ ਤਿਨ ਕਹਾ
Parthame Aonkar Tin Kaha
Aonkar was recited first of all.

ਪ੍ਰਿਥਮੇ ਕਾਲ ਜਬ ਕਰਾ ਪ੍ਰਸਾਰਾ, ਓਅੰਕਾਰ ਤੇ ਸ੍ਰਿਸ਼ਟ ਉਪਾਰਾ
Pritham Kaal Jab Kara Prasara, Oankar Tey Srishat Upara
When the creation started, Aonkar gave rise to the world.

Now the accepted pronunciation is **Ek Aonkar** but some people say that **Ek Ong kar** is the right way.

There are different views about the correct spellings and pronunciation of it. A scholar in a sect called **Eckankar** has given the following versions of **Ek Aonkar**: *Ikk Aunkar, Ikomkar, Ik Onkar, Ek Omkar, Ekk Aum Kar, Ek Aungkar, Ekk Aonkar, Ek Oanikar, Ik Omkara, Ik-oanNkaar. Aykankaru, Aonkarru, Ekomkar, Ekam Onkar, Ekaonkar, EcKankar, Ek oankaar, Eckankar, Ek Ankar, Ekankar, Ekaankar, Ekankarr, Ekangkar, Ekankaar, Ek angkar, Ek ongkar, Ek ongaar, Ekumkaar, Ek oang kar, Eckankar,* and *Ekankar.*

Ek Aonkar is generally translated in English as "God is one" or "One God" but it does not convey the true meanings as per the teachings of the Sikh religion. **Ek Aonkar** represents one unique creator, without a beginning or an end, and the source of all that exists in the universe. A unique absolute Almighty and the Ultimate reality.

The Almighty of Sikhism is not the same as the Christian God so we should translate it as the "Creator is One and Unique", "The sole and unique Supreme being", "the Eternal Reality", and "Ultimate reality", as per the concept in **Gurbani** (the sayings of Gurus). Ultimate reality or eternal reality is something that is superior, final and fundamental power in all reality. Creator (**Karta Purakh,** the timeless who never dies) is a reality, as being beyond time, the eternal and one only without form. Reality has no smell, taste, sound and colour. We cannot recognise reality. Ultimate Reality has so many qualities that we cannot enumerate them. What we call it is the only description of His some qualities.

ਉੱਚ ਅਪਾਰ ਬੇਅੰਤ ਸੁਆਮੀ ਕਉਣੁ ਜਾਣੈ ਗੁਣ ਤੇਰੇ

Ooch Apar Beant Swami Kaun Janey Gun Tere *(802 - 16)*

Great, unlimited, infinite Master, nobody knows your characteristics. The other meaning is One who is with himself, and all in all. It is a universal truth and will be there forever.

Chapter 8
Ek, Aon, Kar
(੧ = ਇੱਕ ੴ = ਉਅੰ + ਕਾਰ)

Ek Aonkar is made of three parts: **Ek**, **Aon**, **Kar**.

Ek is one but here it means *unique*. One is the most auspicious word since ancient time in most of the languages of the world and conveys the idea of a universal force. Number 1 is independent. It is the number of unity which combines all other numbers within it. In Christainty number one symbolizes God. It is the symbol of the singleness, God's unique and universal power. According to Pythagoreans, 1 is not a number at all because number means plurality and 1 is singular. Indian scriptures consider One (**Ek**) as a symbolic representation of the cosmic soul (entire creation) with qualities and form.

ਏਕੁ ਪਿਤਾ ਏਕਸ ਕੇ ਹਮ ਬਾਰਿਕ ਤੂ ਮੇਰਾ ਗੁਰ ਹਾਈ
Ek Pita Ekas Ke Hum Barik Tu Mera Gur Haayee (611 - 19)
We all are children of One Father who is our Spiritual Guide.

Everything can be one but cannot be unique. If we pick an apple out of hundreds, the apple is one but not unique. There may be so many like it. If we take the one as unique then it conveys the idea that He is the only one and there is nothing like Him (creator). Here one is not a mathematical numerical but a universal creative force. It is singular, unique, indivisible, infinite and fathomless. *Ek* existed before time and shall continue to exist when everything else, even time and space has dissolved. The mind alone can never find Him.

This one is also called **Eko**, **Ekas** and **Ekam**. Guru Nanak Dev Ji was of the view that **Eko** represents a unique one master. Guru Arjun Dev ji said, *"By itself this one is just one and only one and is the source of creation."*

According to Bhai Gurdas, by writing one in the beginning of **Aonkar** it has been shown that **Ekankar**, the only one Almighty, has the power.

In **Gurbani** it is further said, *"Ek* represents One (unique) creator, the source of all that exists, without beginning or an end".

ਆਦਿ ਅਨੀਲੁ ਅਨਾਦਿ ਅਨਾਹਤਿ ਜੁਗੁ ਜੁਗੁ ਏਕੋ ਵੇਸੁ
Adi Aneel Anaad Anahat Jug Jug Eko Vase (6 - 17)
**Eternal wind and water have existed
since the very beginning and will continue till the end.**

Ek Aonkar also means the saying of **Ekam**. Sometimes instead of **Ek Aonkar**, **Ekamkar** (**Ekam** + **akar**) is used. **Ekam** is one of the most ancient words used for one in several ancient Indian languages.
- In **Sanskrit** (an Indian language for **Hindu** religion), it means "One, single, solitary, the creative and absolute force in the universe equated with the supreme power in the center of reality".
- In **Tamil** (South Indian language), it means "supreme, ultimate Oneness, which is present everywhere".

It was said that from this **ekam** all objects of the universe were formed. This (One) Creator cannot be compared or contrasted with any other. It is in existence and will continue to exist.

The early symbol of **Ek Aonkar** logo by Sikh Gurus was Punjabi numerical One with **Orah** with a waving top and was called **Eckankar**. Some people consider **Ek Aonkar** as a figure of **Waheguru,** which means the glorified teacher.

The Second part of Ek Aon kar (viz, **Aon)** is represented by **Oorah** sound (O). It represents the one which is limitless. It is a universal ever-flowing divine melody called **anhad naad.** It means the concept of duality, one being a symbol of one's own divinity and the other that of the Creator.

Guru Nanak Dev Ji gave the sermon as follows:

ਉੜੈ ਉਪਮਾ ਤਾ ਕੀ ਕੀਜੈ ਜਾ ਕਾ ਅੰਤ ਨ ਪਾਇਆ

Ooray Upama Taa Kee Keejai Jaa Ka Ant Na Paya *(432 - 12)*
Greatness of Oorah is that it is beyond human comprehension.

The curve on the **Oorah** stresses the long sound of a vowel **Hora.** This long flourish is energy to rise upwards into the infinite. It indicates that it is the **mantra** of ascent and causes devotees to climb on top, what we call **Chardikala.** It connects us with the guidance power of the inner Guru. It gives strength, power, protection and grace. It provides happiness and hope by lifting the mood.

The third part of **Ek Aonkar** is "kar". It is an abbreviation of **akriti** or **akar. Kar** is a never-ending continuation of one constant divine power. It is an image that impresses the mind. It is a mode of mental functioning and events. Some people say **Kar** means **ras** (extract), **seva** (service), to act, to do speech, shape, and sign.

Chapter 9
Nature

Guru Nanak Dev Ji believed that **Onkar** (**Aonkar**) represents nature (**Prakriti**). It can change and is changing. It is animate and inanimate that inhabits the mountains, trees, oceans and deserts.

Nature we see, nature we hear, nature we observe with wonderful joy.
Nature is species, kind, colour, nature is life forms.
Nature is air, water, nature is the soil of the earth.
Nature is real and all comprehension.

ਬਨਿ ਤਿਨਿ ਪਰਬਤਿ ਹੈ ਪਾਰਬ੍ਰਹਮੁ
Ban Tin Parbat Hai Paar Braham (294 - 1)
**The forests, fields and mountains are Par Brahman
(Akal Purakh, beyond description).**

Chapter 10
Basic Tenets of Guru Nanak Dev Ji

After His extensive academic travels, Guru Nanak Dev Ji settled in Kartarpur on the bank of river Ravi which is now in Pakistan but is connected with Indian Punjab by a corridor. He gave sermons and advised local people on the right way of living. He laid stress on understanding His teachings and following them instead of performing the rituals. These were later incorporated by Guru Arjun Dev Ji in **Sri Guru Granth Sahib Ji.**

Ek Aonkar is the conclusion of the lifelong learning (thesis) of Guru Nanak Dev Ji. He laid stress on working hard (**Kirat Karo**), meditation (**Naam Japo**) and sharing worldly possessions with the needy (**Vand Chako**). During His last stages, He set an example for others by working in the fields, meditating and distributing the fruits of His labor (**langar** community kitchen) to the others.

ਸਚਹੁ ਓਰੈ ਸਭੁ ਕੋ ਉਪਰਿ ਸਚੁ ਆਚਾਰੁ

Sachay Ure Sabh Ko Upar Sach Aachar (62 - 11)

Truth is higher than everything but truthful living is higher than it.

Gurudwara Kartarpur Sahib

Chapter 11
Simran (Recitation of Ek Aonkar)

Ek Aonkar can be recited in several ways during recitation. Its sound creates a vibration in the body which calms the mind. With the repetition of this **mantra** and listening to one's own voice, thoughts are reduced and the mind rises above materialism. Everyone can use it at any time and at any place.

First Way:

- One is to press the thumb and tip of the pinky finger by saying **Ek**.
- The second is to press the thumb and tip of the ringman finger by saying **Aon**.
- The third is to press the thumb and tip of the tall man's finger by saying **Ka**.
- Fourth is to press the thumb and tip of the pointer finger by saying **Ar**.

  Researchers have confirmed that this exercise helps in the development of the brain.

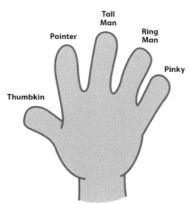

Second way:

- Sit comfortably with eyes closed and inhale saying **Ekum**
- Hold your breath for 30 second
- Exhale slowly saying **Onkar**

Third way:

- Close right nostril with the thumb
- Repeat all the steps as above in the left nostril

Fourth way:

- Close left nostril with the thumb
- Repeat all the steps in the right nostril

Test your Comprehension

1. <u>Guru Nanak Dev Ji</u>:
   - What was Guru Nanak Dev Ji curious about?
   - What are the different forms of studies that Guru Nanak Dev Ji did to learn about the mystery of the Creator?
2. <u>Ek Aonkar</u>:
   - Explain in your own words the meaning of Ek Aonkar.
   - What are the various parts of Ek Aonkar? What does each part stand for?
3. <u>Informational</u>:
   - List at least 3 pronunciations of Ek Aonkar?
   - Where is Kartarpur Sahib located? Why is it important to Sikhs?
   - Who was Bhai Mardana? What instrument did he play? Which musical instrument do you like to play?
4. <u>Application to daily life</u>:
   - Pick one of the meditation forms suggested in the book and do it daily for a week.
   - How will you apply the meaning of Ek Aonkar in your daily life?
   - What did you learn from the life of Guru Nanak Dev Ji? How will you apply these learnings in your daily life?
5. <u>Research</u>:
   - How would you write without any electronic device (e.g. computer, laptop, typewriter, etc) or pen or paper?
   - Pick a topic that you are curious about. Do some research on it. Draw a conclusion.
   - Open-ended feedback for the author:
     - What did you like the most about the book?
     - What suggestions do you have for the author to further improve the book?

You can email the author at *hello@ekaonkar.org*

Acknowledgement

This Children's Book is based on the article *Ek Aonkar* from the book "*Om (Aum) Omkar and Ek Aonkar*" by Dr. H.S. Puri. The book is available at Amazon in both online and in book form.

Thanks are due to the authors of the various websites of Wikipedia, Wikimedia, and following ones:

- http://malicethoughts.blogspot.com/2016/01/sanskrit-or-punjabi.html
- http://Sadhsangat.com
- http://Sikhri.org
- http://Srigranth.org
- http://www.erinmclaughlin.com/hindirinny/2010/12/mool-mantar/
- https://en.wikipedia.org/wiki/File:Guru_Granth_Sahib_By_Bhai_Pratap_Singh_Giani.jpg
- https://en.wikipedia.org/wiki/File:Long_version_Mul_Mantar,_Darshan_Deori,_Golden_Temple.jpg
- https://en.wikipedia.org/wiki/File:Sri_Guru_Granth_Sahib_Nishan.jpg
- https://en.wikipedia.org/wiki/Ik_Onkar
- https://en.wikipedia.org/wiki/Mul_Mantar
- https://sikhspirit.com/punjabi-or-gurmukhi/
- https://www.sikhiwiki.org/index.php/Handwrittens_of_Gurus_period
- https://www.sikhsangat.com/index.php?/topic/13428-omn-vs-waheguru/
- https://www.theworldsikhnews.com/guru-nanaks-acrostics-of-the-35-alphabets-of-punjabi/

Made in the USA
Las Vegas, NV
12 July 2021